the ultimate

500-QUESTION POLITICS AND HISTORY QUIZ

the ultimate

500-QUESTION POLITICS AND HISTORY QUIZ

Tim Bourke

William Scally

LITTLEMORE PRESS

First Published by
Littlemore Press, Dublin, 2021

ISBN 978-1-3999-1136-8

Images: *Adobe Photo Stock*

Table of Contents

Introduction

In the dark days of Covid time, confined to quarters in lockdown, the authors, William Scally and Tim Bourke retained their sanity by engaging in what proved to be an all-engrossing albeit quite mutually competitive enterprise.

The Ultimate 500-Question Politics and History Quiz contains five hundred questions together with their solutions. The questions traverse the world of politics and history and offer the reader what could be described as a rather testing mental workout. Ireland is the main focus of the questions; Britain, Continental Europe and North America figure significantly.

Some of the quiz questions are relatively straightforward; many are quite thought-provoking, including a number that have more than one correct answer. Others are cryptic or constructed with a play on words – even knowledge of the alphabet would not go astray! They require some imagination and lateral thinking. The solutions, however, discreetly located at the back of the book, provide instant relief for the perplexed or mind-boggled.

The Ultimate 500-Question Politics and History Quiz is for those who enjoy flexing their mental muscles. It is versatile and can be enjoyed by oneself or in the company of family and friends. However it is engaged with, it is guaranteed to provoke, frustrate, exercise, irritate, satisfy, please, and, above all, to provide fun and entertainment.

How to

One number in brackets after the question indicates the number of letters in the answer;

A series of numbers indicates the number of letters in each word, if more than one word in the answer;

One number and an apostrophe indicates the traditional Irish name format, O' as in, O'Dea;

the ultimate

500-QUESTION
POLITICS AND HISTORY
QUIZ

SECTION ONE: QUESTIONS

QUESTIONS
01-100

01-100

1. Uneasy lies the head that wears a _____ . (5)

2. Would Pat and Anne favour proper hare coursing, at least in the West? (8)

3. First Irish Chancellor of an African University: a) Name? (5, 6, 1'5) b) Appointed by this post-independence President? (5, 7) c) Location? (5)

4. A Karlsruhe 2020 verdict should put more than Madame _____ on guard. (7)

5. Igloo? (3, 5, 5)

6. Great saint brought warmth and comfort to the lost, trapped and bewildered, including in North Kildare. (7)

7. In the past, _____ preceded Gregorian but later, Brandon followed _____ . (6)

8. Like an Odearest, well sprung by Sean Bourke? (6, 5)

9. Proinsias, Wilbur, Shane; politically not much in common? (4)

10. Carrie _____ , out East, not for the slaughter. (3)

11. Left his mainstream UK Party a few years ago, not chucked out, but to no avail. (6)

12. Journalists or commentators: _____ get a political party? Fintan _____; _____ Power; _____ Mullaly; _____ Lawlor; _____ Marlowe; _____ Peston. (6)

13. Not remembered as Maid Marian in UK? (8, 8)

14. Alleged heretic and later saint, she had an indiscreet stakeout, by the sound of it. (4, 2, 3)

15. Elected to the Second Chamber in 2020, but surely it was not her plan. (4, 8)

16. He seems to bloom in the Seanad. (5, 6)

17. One-time British Labour leader could talk the talk, and indeed was christened in honour of an Irish patriot, but did he walk the walk? (7, 4)

18. Paid a heavy price for such over confidence, not in the Crucible, but, shortly afterwards in the U.K. election. (4, 7)

19. Prime Minister once seen as a liberalising reformer, but now signs of ethnic and nationalist mode. (4)

20. In the long run, we are all dead. (4, 7, 6)

21. In France, niece Marion _____ dropped a name – maybe with the stroke of a pen. (8)

22. Get a leading international organisation from these three current UK MPs? _____ Dowden (Conservative); Claire _____ (SDLP); _____ Hobhouse (Liberal Democrat). (3)

23. She had an awful temper, but only once lost the head, in public. (4, 6)

24. In their well-known roles as journalists or commentators, odd person out? _____ Boulton; _____ Blitzer; Andrew _____ ; _____ Corcoran. (4)

25. Nigel and Diane have had their ups and downs, and now, apparently also _____ . (9)

26. A briar pipe: he used this to charm and, arguably, deceive a nation! (6, 6)

27. When these 3 musketeers left college in Cork for Dublin flatland and other distractions, sometimes there was no room at the inn. (8 and 7 and 1'5)

28. In their day, Tony and Dick often sounded very angry! (8, 8)

29. AA, an African Prime Minister, but not in the AA breakdown service. (4, 5)

30. "The barbers are open in _____ " Dáil remark June 2020. (7)

31. In the Cliveden set, it sounds like he was for, not against, this noxious emission. (4, 7)

32. Later, naval commander and Lord, in earlier guise, had to batten down the hatches after hitting an iceberg. (5, 11)

33. A big 'gamble' for just five votes. (6)

34. Ivan, Ivana, or Ivanka _____ find the second name of the one with a current electoral mandate. (5)

35. Two "nice" boys from the East End with political connections were "this pair".
(3, 4, 5)

36. Get a political party: (4, 4) _____ Maitlis; _____ Emerson; _____ Oakeshott; Fergus _____ ; _____ Harris; _____ Kerrigan; _____ Pierce; _____ Kuenssberg.

37. To be frank about it, knighted and later stripped – in art, he 'kept' very well under the circumstances. (7, 5)

38. Still around, not a real queen herself, and not Pearse. (6)

39. One-time important political adviser, but not to Fianna Fail or Fine Gael. (6, 6)

40. Athlone politician and Chinese rebellion. (5)

41. More Dunganstown than Castleross. (3, 8)

42. Was his masterpiece belligerent or pacific or indeed both? (3, 7)

43. Welsh wife Penelope and children filled posts, if not jobs. (6)

44. What kind of headgear were these two wearing, by the sound of them? (7, 4)

45. His scratch on a Cabra Bridge led to a technology revolution. (7, 5, 8)

46. Past VP is part of L.S.D. (5)

47. He cast a cold eye on life and death. (7, 6, 5)

48. This quartet of 'horsemen' tried to do us proud. (5, 7, 1'5, 8)

49. Never quite made the FG first team, but later a long time on the bench. (6, 10)

50. An oft-quoted existentialist question? (2, 2, 2, 3, 2, 2)

51. Odd man out, as never back in: Lynch, Cowen, Ahern, Kenny? (5)

52. Once held in major IRA escapade, now in gyms, not shops. (3, 5)

53. Were these two the meat in the Brezhnev-Gorbachev sandwich? (8, 9)

54. On Northern Ireland, Basil and decades later Peter differed, to put it mildly. (6)

55. Far away east, after sunset, can you bank on _____ being "in"? (4)

56. Big change up North in this constituency in 1983. (4, 7)

57. One-time US presidential candidate, not a silver liquid! (9)

58. Amber is a type of 'blue', but far away Kevin was a type of 'amber'! (4)

59. Entitled to self-nominate for next Irish presidential election. (8)

60. Ministerial Helen close enough to Minister of State _____ , at least in constituency terms. (4)

61. Did these upwardly mobile Irish-Americans in the 1980s bite the hand that fed them? (6, 9)

62. This bird was quite feminine. (8, 7)

63. After getting the top job, this "son of the manse" was caught in two minds, apparently. (6, 5)

64. In the cold war era, a successful defence of his title against him, who sounds like the son of Steven. (10)

65. Did he flower in Dublin? (7, 5)

66. As a mad bull, he was, by the sound of him, noted by name for this tendency (but not in a Spanish context). (7, 7) or (7, 6) - both are correct.

67. This president is not from a street area now centred on 'Connolly', but from elsewhere. (8, 6)

68. Before: _____ Paisley; _____ Robinson; _____ Foster. Outcome is: research, analysis, information, diary. (3)

69. This west of Ireland family, in the past, featured in both UK and Irish politics. (6)

70. Noted for her caviar? (6, 8)

71. Did this major US clean-sweeping politician operate in a vacuum? (7, 6)

72. Was Stan Laurel's partner, however distantly, related to this early Labour leader? (4, 6)

73. B, A, L, T: Johnsons past and present; two of them with a similar political ideology. (4, 3)

74. "Juan's gal". (5)

75. A very provincial dwelling. (8, 5)

76. Did this Italian take the biscuit? (9)

77. Was this a job for the Roncalli and Pacelli boys? (4)

78. One common factor at least: Ferris; Vincent P.; O'Donoghue; Catherine; Cullen; Mansergh; Michael; Heydon; Kenny. (6)

79. In vehicular propulsion terms (and sounds), the GOP had a Lincoln, and then got him. (6, 4)

80. The lad has done well by Cornwall. (6, 7)

81. "Ich bin ein Berliner." (4, 1, 7)

82. Was this academic also a locksmith? (5, 5)

83. Was he responsible for the betrayal of Christ in Leeson Street? (10)

84. It has been argued that this Italian political group is quite backward. (5, 6)

85. One was king, another kaiser, and a third, tsar. Relatively speaking, what were they in common? (7)

86. At least in theory, he was in pursuit of justice. (4, 5)

87. AJF O'Reilly once suggested that the distinguishing feature of the Irish Co-Operative Movement was _____ . (3, 7, 2, 11)

88. This Minister, some decades ago, "bought" the wrong footwear! (4, 6)

89. Did this Englishman revert to Down in his pursuit of a past colonial vision? (5, 6)

90. Major Irish office holders: G, then W, then another W, and then G again. Name G. (9)

91. There was Declan (then) and Patrick (now) and in between there was _____ . (3)

92. Capital, but not Atlanta? (7)

93. In a part of Leinster, _____ is a T.D. (7)

94. These papers went down like a bombshell in America, SE Asia and beyond. (3, 8)

95. If Tet was the military game changer in Vietnam, this massacre was the public opinion one. (2, 3)

96. The over-arching US rationale informing the Vietnam war was known as _____ _____ _____ . (3, 6, 6)

97. This one-time staff sergeant in the US army kept a terrible secret about his work in South East Asia. (5, 9)

98. A strategic overview, from the Hellfire Club. (3, 8, 8)

99. The political and institutional structures underpinning the framework documents leading to the "Good Friday" (Belfast) Agreement. Strand 1; (8) Strand 2; (5-5) Strand 3. (4-4)

100. This Saorstát Minister reduced the old age pension from 10 shillings to 9 shillings a week. (6, 6)

QUESTIONS
101-200

101-200

101. This Vladimir was put in but not put out. (5)

102. Not John Rawls, this tract proved influential for a time in some party circles here. (7, 1, 4, 7)

103. Get a former Lord Mayor and prominent Green politician, though not yet in the league below: (3) _____ von der Leyen; (6) Simon _____ ; (7) Simon _____ . (6)

104. Lawyer, office holder in Irish politics and academic who wrote robustly about the Constitution. (4, 5)

105. In the opinion of many, in high office she was 'supremely' able. (5, 6)

106. "Even Russia, which is a _____ country, has its pubs open." (Michael Collins TD, on RTE 1/9/2020) (9)

107. "He had a large 'army', mainly drawn from the civilian population, affectionately known as _____ army. (5's)

108. This game for ruffians knew no boundaries. (5)

109. Ironically, many thought he fell short. (3, 4, 6)

110. Was this member of the Irish Senate at various times in the 1920's, 1930's and early 1940's known for body odour? (12)

111. He was often at large. (3, 3, 6)

112. Are they all interested in the rights of man? Q _____ non, The Friendly Sons of St. _____ _____ Rebellion, The _____ Freedom Party, British _____ Party. (5)

113. There was the "beef" between these two guys. (8, 1'6)

114. Certainly not a dodo; knew well how to win a presidency in 2020. (4)

115. This nationality not known for lawsuits. (3, 5)

116. A porcine view to rival Naples or San Francisco. (3, 3, 2, 4)

117. Broadcasters/presenters: get one of their own, but look to France. (6)

_____ McCullagh; (5) Robert _____ ; (6) _____ Tubridy; (4) Christiane _____ ; (8) _____ Dale; (4) _____ Byrne. (6)

118. Was he ahead of his Times? (7, 6)

119. Headline: "Dewey defeats Truman". (7, 5, 7)

120. This chap seemed to be chained to his office for an age. (5, 5)

121. It was said to be the year of the French, but at the end of the day, they really were not at these races. (9)

122. His reputation never fully recovered from that "appalling vista". (7)

123. "The lads" as Aidan O'Brien would say (there are three of them), will decide. But what about our lads? ECMONEAHLAMEIOL? (7, 3, 5)

124. A long time ago, he became very notable for his promissory notes. (4, 3)

125. It can be argued of this renowned Irish institution that, by and large, it took the King's shilling. (7's, 10)

126. Philosopher and economist, neo-classical, a rival to Keynes. (9, 3, 5)

127. This Irish civil servant of old, sounded like she enjoyed a pint. (6, 5)

128. Was he the first man of Israel? (5, 3, 6)

129. This man from the South Circular Road area in Dublin was in his time a successor of Moses. (5, 6)

130. This guy fought like he had not a patch on his trousers, wherever else. (5, 5)

131. Did a miscarriage of justice arise from taking this line? (3, 7, 5, 7)

132. Many thought that on the floor, he resembled "Dennis the Menace". (7)

133. He sailed as if on a cloud. (6, 5)

134. This first lady, over thirty years ago, not only reached the summit but, by all accounts, conquered it: a) Who? (5, 9) b) Where? (9)

135. These postmen were kept going by a sore throat. (8, 9)

136. Yet another postman, but definitely not "Big Ben". (3, 7)

137. This businesswoman and parliamentarian in Britain (deceased 2021) came from Cork. (5, 1', 7)

138. Get the missing EU Commissioner's initials from Ireland since 1985: RMcS; PH; CMcC; PF; PS; MMcG; MG-Q. (2)

139. "It's like being savaged by a dead sheep". Who said this? (5, 6) About whom? (8, 4)

140. A Crown Court now sits in this former "priest ridden" town. (7)

141. In the news (2020-2021): Get politician assassinated in 1922. (5) Alexander _____ ; (10) _____ Ryan; (5) Phil _____ ; (5) Rishi _____ ; (5) Shinzo _____ . (3)

142. Political slogans: find the correct years: a) "There is an alternative" _____ b) "Time for change" _____ c) "A lot done. More to do." _____ d) "Let Lemass lead on _____ ".

143. Was also Emmanuel, but in the Commons, not the Elysée. (8)

144. The Pope sometimes speaks *urbi et orbi*, but this long-serving prime minister speaks for a view of where his country should stand. (5)

145. International organisations or agencies: get a Special Administrative Region in a very large country (5): F_O; N_TO; _NICEF; I_F, OE_D

146. Name the political leaders who said: a) "Stand back and stand by". (6, 1, 5); b) "As a community, we are living beyond our means". (7, 1, 7)

147. Like Pope Leo XIII, this European was a champion of subsidiaries. (7, 6)

148. Labour MP married to former Prime Minister of which country? (7)

149. The demonised name the US military used for the Vietnamese enemy. (5)

150. John McCain et al "resided" in this POW camp, widely known as _____   _____   _____ . (3, 5, 6)

151. Did this car manufacturer lose his drive over Vietnam? (6, 8)

152. Sometime in the future, will she be thinking of Ramsay? (4, 3)

153. The Soviet, or perhaps the Irish, "green" movement. (8)

154. Academic and Scottish MP in the last century; wrote an important book on British cabinet government. (4,10)

155. A pressing matter: a) several centuries ago; (3, 9, 8, 5) b) A far later British copycat. (9).

156. The principle of subsidiarity was more or less mooted in this Papal Encyclical. (In Latin; 5, 7)

157. There may well be more "orangemen" within this Spanish city than in Belfast. (7)

158. "There are not two Germanys, a good one and a bad one, but only one, whose best turned into evil through devilish cunning". Who said it? (6, 4)

159. "It's the economy, stupid!" Who coined this phrase? (5, 8)

160. Who was the last king of the peacocks? (4, 2, 4)

161. Unlike Saul of Tarsus, he does not seem to have had a Damascene conversion. (6, 2, 5)

162. It was not to be the Garden of Eden. (4, 5)

163. "Vive la _____ Libre!" (De Gaulle 1967) (6)

164. He was in the Congress for many years, but not in the USA. (6,5)

165. Would this "beacon" of empire, if he had been alive, have written a biography of Philby? (7, 7)

166. Syrian port, with its access to the Mediterranean, provides the main strategic rationale for Russian "interest" in Syria. (6)

167. This north western Syrian port city on the Mediterranean and its hinterland is Al-Assad's home base. (7)

168. The name of Al-Assad's minority Shia sect is _____ ? (7)

169. This Academy sounds like an Italian river. (8, 2)

170. A haughtier version of the IPA. (5, 9, 1'14)

171. A University founded under Royal Charter in 1592. (7, 7, 6)

172. Was this a "method of indoctrination" before its time? (3, 8, 2, 10)

173. From a French viewpoint, was this the end of the world? (10)

174. This Antipodean was more than birdlike, in or out of office. (3,5)

175. The model T gave rise to this 'ism'. (7)

176. Abdel was his middle name. (6)

177. Good heights from which to keep an eye on the natives. (5)

178. Is it easy to fall in this African capital? (7)

179. Some 30 years ago, who said "Well Mr. Collins, tell us (the Speaker's Cabinet) how you (the EU) propose to solve our problems". (1, 1, 2, 5)

180. Somewhat like a quantum physics puzzle, this College is both in Cambridge and not in Cambridge. (7)

181. OMAL, anagram for short name for current President of _____ . (6)

182. Michael and Mattie very much still there, but _____ has gone. (6)

183. Which Irish Dail constituency has three grass race tracks. (9)

184. Cathal in Clare, Ollie around Galway, and Sean in Dublin would never pass _____ laws. (3, 4)

185. He was 'King of the Castle' for a long time, but well north west of Monaghan. (4, 6)

186. Irish politician who tasted a variety of exotic leaves in his day. (5, 5)

187. Some 30 years ago, his swansong in U.K politics was on late Irish telly? (5, 6)

188. "Red Club", get a State capital in a southern US state. (5, 5)

189. A Brigham Young alumnus, one-time Governor of Massachusetts and Presidential candidate and now US Senator. (4, 6)

190. Irish think-tanks most unlikely to be doing what the answer does! (3) ESR _____ ; TAS _____ ; IIE_____.

191. From a long way back: "expense, and great expense may be an essential part in true economy". (6, 5)

192. A continental considered fond of good wine but not necessarily of junkets. (7)

193. Which Taoiseach during his period of office was involved with four different Presidents? (8)

194. Which President during his periods of office was involved with four different Taoisigh? (7)

195. Two birds: IBONR Swann (MLA) (5) Angela EEGAL (MP) (5)

196. This State is foreign in America. (3, 5, 10)

197. Boys from Drimnagh who climbed to the top of the political ladder? (5, 3)

198. Even Hamburgers agree that this is the paper of record. (11, 10, 7)

199. This German politician proved to be "great gas". (7, 8) or (7, 9) are both correct.

200. He was a long serving guardian of the people, mainly in the British Isles. (4, 11)

QUESTIONS
201-300

201-300

201. Posted up North. (7, 4, 6)

202. Although its readership, up North, may be distressed to hear it, not quite Home Counties material. (3, 7, 9)

203. Celtic propaganda? (3, 5, 4)

204. "Lord, make me pure, but not yet." To whom is this aspiration attributed? (2, 9)

205. Five proofs for the existence of God. Who formulated them? (2, 6, 7)

206. He "christianised" Rome. (11)

207. He succeeded Adenauer. (6, 6)

208. He preceded Valéry Giscard d'Estaing. (7, 8)

209. He succeeded Franco. (4, 4, 6)

210. You can't hold the Easter candle to him. (7, 7)

211. About two centuries ago, he made a useful contribution to economic and political theory. (6, 7)

212. He wrote this economic treatise without the help of Eve. The book (3, 6, 2, 7); the author. (4, 5)

213. This Shannonside lad, was a tribune all unto himself. (7,6)

214. This magazine was typically "hot off the presses". (3, 5)

215. This magazine had a weekly satirical column by "Denis" on life with "Margaret". (7, 3) What was the name of the weekly column in question? (4, 4)

216. RTE commentator on the funeral of JFK (7, 1'5)

217. The longest-serving broadcaster in RTE (4, 6)

218. He became synonymous with the election (British general) "swingometer". (5, 4)

219. Was this former Prime Minister of Canada the son of a lord by the sound of him? (6,7)

220. This leading Nazi was the recording secretary at the notorious "final solution" Wansee Conference (5, 8)

221. Who tracked down Eichmann in South America nearly two decades   after the war, whereby he was abducted by Mossad to meet his fate in Israel. (5,10)

222. Key Nazi leader assassinated in Czechoslovakia in 1942. (8, 8)

223. Chinese philosopher of great significance. (9)

224. The greatest of the Chinese dynasties? (3)

225. The political governance concept of "the Aireacht" made its debut in this late-sixties reform proposal. (3, 6, 6)

226. At the mines in the 1980s, he argued until he was blue in the face. (6, 8)

227. Back in the day, a Donegal Ceann Comhairle. (6, 7)

228. A dog's breakfast but, pre-Covid, a staple media item, and lingers on. (6)

229. It can truly be said that he played senior hurling, whatever about Michael. (7, 4)

230. Became a well-known, indeed famous building associate of Bertie's. (5, 3, 9)

231. Assassinated: _____ Lumumba; _____ Palme; Leon, _____; _____ Franz Ferdinand; Abraham _____ . Then get a major political philosopher. (5)

232. "That's capital, Wilmington, my dear fellow!" (8)

233. Although he was on the rocks towards the end, he made the bay his own. (4, 6)

234. Were his hands tied during the Falklands war? (4, 4)

235. This former famous US broadcaster sounded like he was made of cement. (6, 8)

236. He wrote a letter home every week. (8, 5)

237. Michael Mills, David Thornley, Michael McInerney, among others, did not play this game, but were participants, nonetheless. (3, 7, 2, 3, 5)

238. A doctor in charge in the House, in his day. (4, 1'6)

239. "Every Prime Minister needs a Willie." To whom was Margaret Thatcher referring? (6, 8)

240. "I grew up in the 30's with an unemployed father. He didn't riot. He got on his bike and looked for work, and he kept looking until he found it". (6, 6)

241. She was the only public figure of her sex to officially greet JFK in Ireland. (7, 7)

242. She was the first woman to contest a constitutional   case on contraception in Ireland. It became known as the _____ case. (5)

243. Scottish leader of a Labour Party in his day. (5, 8)

244. When he got stranded, had he a case to answer? (5, 8)

245. Seoirse Beag O Cymru? (5, 6)

246. Was Pakistan's capital, from "independence" to the mid-eighties. (7)

247. Currently, capital of Pakistan. (9)

248. Bangladesh, formerly known (post independence) as _____ . (4, 8)

249. Regarded as the first modern book on elections; in this case the 1960 US presidential election: a) the book. (3, 6, 2, 3, 9); b) the author. (8, 1, 5)

250. He was the 'John Charles McQuaid' of Melbourne back in the day. (10, 6)

251. This Killane boy was wanted in Australia for disturbing the peace. (3, 5)

252. He led Australia to the brink of becoming a republic. (4, 7)

253. The major European powers conference in 1881 to divide up Africa, was held in this city. (6)

254. "The fools! The fools, they have left us our Fenian dead, and Ireland unfree shall never be at peace." Who was the orator? (7, 6)

255. Party leaders (2021 going back): S, C, M, B, B. Fill in the first initial of the surname of the preceding leader. (1)

256. Served as inaugural First Minister of Scotland. (6, 5)

257. Neil Kinnock's Welsh political inspiration. (7, 5)

258. This former MLA was not at Trafalgar. (6, 10)

259. Conor's book on Kitty's boyfriend? (7, 3, 3, 5)

260. Still 'sitting' _____ after UK Cabinet reshuffle in September 2021. (5)

261. This Tammany Hall demagogue was not selected for the All-Ireland final. (4, 6)

262. He was the first catholic candidate in a US presidential election. (2, 5)

263. An 'Irish' city in old Montana! (5)

264. He got a job, out of the blue, in Foreign Affairs, but he stayed in the same House. (3, 5)

265. This Anglo-French agreement after World War 1 neatly produced two new "desert" states. (5, 5)

266. With the assistance of the Anglo Iranian oil company, this democratically elected chap was ousted in a coup d'état. (9)

267. She was the first black US ambassador. (7, 6, 5)

268. Not Vladimir, but did this man have monarchical tendencies_____ ? (8)

269. Murderer/assassin in the theatre. (4, 6, 5)

270. Murdered/assassinated in the cathedral. (6, 1, 6)

271. Dedicated to (failed) assassination attempts on Charles de Gaulle. Nickname? (3, 6)

272. *The Third Man*, who was a master of this and other spy novels and film screenplays? (6, 6)

273. He's in the wrong lands, but "mark" my words, he would drink in the Stag's Head if he could. (4, 5)

274. This "piggy bank" that our viking relatives filled, sounds regal. (9, 6, 4)

275. This chap was not actually stationed in Finland. (5)

276. A teutonic slice of stale danish pastry? (9, 8)

277. Despite central heating, double-glazing etc., it sounds a very "draughty" place. (8)

278. This place in Madrid in the 1980's seemed offensive to some Francoists. (3, 6)

279. In the opinion of some, does this French address now signify a counter-revolution? (3, 6, 6)

280. A Doctor's son from Hispaniola. (4, 3, 8)

281. This chap was head of the Dominicans, over half a century ago. (6, 8)

282. Successful Prime Minister, for the first few years at least: ANAERIDDJNACR. (7, 6)

283. Herbert did not make it in the UK after World War II, but is now the man Down Under. (5)

284. Later, Michael did not make it either in the UK, but _____ did in the past Down Under. (4)

285. World Trade Organisation: a) First Director (1995) Peter _____; (10) b) New Director General (March 2021); Ngozi _____ _____ . (6, 6)

286. Four large Irish lakes: Get a currency first and follow with the name of a US Senator. (4, 4)

287. New MP from Northern Ireland in 2019: STEMUOLCOWADO. (5, 8)

288. Wisdom? a) to throw snowballs at Lord _____ ; (5) b) to play table tennis with Xi _____ . (8)

289. This pair, in early 2021, sounded like fish in hot water. (8, 7)

290. GBS and the Webb-Ellis's were founder members of this group. (3, 6, 7)

291. This German introduced social policy to modern governance. (8)

292. *War and Social Policy* author. (7, 7)

293. In May 2021, up North, sounded like he undermined British Telecom with a shovel. (4, 7)

294. John Reidy wrote the ground-breaking score for this film. (4, 4)

295. The Irishman who wrote the book/screenplay for this *Longest Day*? (9, 4)

296. Rivers: Match with an appropriate constituency TD beginning with the same letter: Boyne (5); Corrib (8); Liffey outside Dublin (7); Dargle (8).

297. In the Indian Ocean, in unity for a long time with the "home country"! (7)

298. Henry Kenny's Fianna Fáil football counterpart? (4, 8)

299. What additional name does this Donegal politician have? (3, 4)

300. Came full belt on to the yellowbellies, and later to Europe. (5, 5)

QUESTIONS
301-400

301. This TD (deceased) played a hurling and football final in Croke Park on the same day. (3, 5)

302. "There was a sound of revelry by night, and _____ capital had gathered then her beauty and her chivalry": a) What country? (7) b) Before what battle? (8)

303. All past in Laois-Offaly, get a Green Party office holder: Brian _____ ; _____ Parlon; Olwyn _____ ; _____ O'Higgins; _____ Enright; William _____ ; Liam _____ ? (7)

304. This leader looked as if he cast a cold eye on life, whatever about death, and was for many, in thought and deed the ultimate symbol of the Cold War. (6, 8)

305. His diplomatic approach was blown to pieces. (11, 5, 5)

306. This hostelry's famous speciality of the house was at times *la Bombe Surprise*. (3, 6)

307. Over 20 years ago, he walked out of Castle Buildings in the name of democracy. (7, 9)

308. He understood the art and science of the "D, L/D" gerrymander better than most. (5, 7)

309. As one now remembers, they were all getting peerages hand over fist, then this Taig gets one and the tone is irrevocably altered! (5, 4)

310. Loyalists could not, at one point, beat a single drum on this road. (8)

311. Did he suffer from Stockhausen's Syndrome at Monasterevin? (5, 7)

312. Not quite "ashes to ashes" when she was in charge! (4, 3, 3)

313. Two former UK Prime Ministers: Match with these two constituencies. Sedgefield _____ (5); Huntingdon _____ . (5)

314. The Indian Machiavelli _____ (8) wrote his science of politics _____ (12) about 1800 years before *The Prince*.

315. Not on the Costa del Sol, but the Prime Minister of this country is not far away. (8)

316.   Political parties in Germany and France: from the first letter of any word in each party's name, get an Irish Taoiseach: (6) LA REPUBLIQUE EN MARCHE, AFD, SPD, DEMOCRATIC MOVEMENT, SOCIALIST PARTY, DIE LINKE

317.   Away far north: a) a 'Nordic Merkel' defeated in 2021 _____ NERA LOGBERS; (4,7) b) "the youngest female state leader" NASNA ARIMN. (5, 5)

318.   A traditional mode: Sweden, Spain, United Kingdom, Norway, Netherlands, Denmark: a) The mode? (8) and b) add an appropriate European country. (7)

319.   "The Northern Ireland protocol is a dagger at the heart of the Union": One-time UUP leader on 1/1/21. (3, 5)

320.   Where did Ireland rank in the UN Human Development Index 2019-2020 data? Was it 127th, or 60th or 17th, or 5th or 2nd ?

321.   USA has recognised Moroccan control over: a) what country? (7, 6) b) Against the wishes of what people? (7)

322. Sons-in-law and daughter-in-law also held political office; outcome is a very important court: Sean Lemass, _____ Garret FitzGerald, _____ Michael Pat Murphy, _____ . (3)

323. Once Parliamentary Secretaries and all Ireland football medallists: sons achieved higher office. (5, 6)

324. _____ liver salts still in stock in Dublin! (7)

325. Slogan: "The straight vote is crooked." Name the year. (4)

326. Stalin: a) Daughter: first name; (8) b) Lead military commander: surname? (6) c) Stalin's successor: first name and surname? (6, 8)

327. Churchill: a) Son; (8) b) Wife; (10) c) Childhood residence; (8, 6) d) Adult residence? (9)

328. This Greek philosopher drank himself to death. (8)

329. Author of *The Open Society and its Enemies*. (4, 6)

330. The Spandau Two? (4, 5)

331. This chap developed his skills in Spanish Morocco, and then honed them in his own country. (6)

332. In the last century, this African monarch had real staying power. (6)

333. He has 'modest holdings' in the South West of England. (6, 7)

334. Vietnam War: a) the changing offensive; (3) b) the North Vietnamese army chief. (4)

335. The French imperial project came to an end at this battle. (4, 4, 3)

336. Commander of American forces in Vietnam for most of the war. (12)

337. These brothers did the Pentagon no favours. (3, 9)

338. Was this prominent Vietnamese lady new to the job by the sound of her? (6, 3)

339. This chap was "lynched" in the 1940s, but not in the American south. (2, 4)

340. What does Abuja have in common with Brasilia? (8)

341. Was he a violinist in Rome's olden days? (4)

342. Sounds like he's from Russia. Indeed, if he exists at all, Lenin and co. would have denounced him as a "Rightist". (9, 7)

343. Away out East, was he a case of calling the kettle black? (3, 3)

344. "Was this Iberian judicial process
unduly inquisitive?
(3, 7, 11)

345. One-time US Secretary of State could work in the dark! (8)

346. One-time members of the Dáil: Johnny, Billy, Mildred. (3)

347. This "red army" excelled in urban-rural re-alignment. (5, 5)

348. Labour's Churchill? (6, 5)

349. Recently deceased spy writer under this *nom-de-plume*. (4, 2, 5)

350. Now the FSB, before that the KGB and before that the NKVD, but what preceded these three? (3, 5)

351. Tully may have ducked in time, but this prominent leader had no chance. (5, 5)

352. Was this "foreigner" noted for mixing his drinks? (7)

353. This much-referred to work landed in Ireland in the seventies, but its findings hardly saw the light of day. (3, 5, 6)

354. "Labour owed more to Methodism than to Marx". Who proposed this idea? (5, 6)

355. Echoes of the Turkish genocide of Armenians in the early 20th century have recently resounded, (mainly by proxy): a) where? (7, 8) b) the proxy? (10)

356. The Islamic tradition that holds the Saudi system together is called _____ ? (9)

357. This Saudi company is the world's largest oil company. (6)

358. It is widely assumed, but as yet unproven, that this lad plotted the killing of Jamal Khashoggi in Istanbul (initials only). (3)

359. The Commission for the Promotion of Virtue and the Prevention of Vice is the watchdog of the Wahhabi doctrine. Who enforces it? (3, 9, 6)

360. Author of: a) *The Great Hunger.* (5,7-5) and b) *Ireland since the Famine*"? (1, 1, 1, 5)

361. Did Tim Pat Coogan's mother blow this up? (3, 3, 4)

362. An Orwellian quintet: a) Did he pay "Homage" to this place? _____ ; (9) b) Tyranny in a rural setting? (6, 4) c) Was this work out of date? (4) d) The road to here was definitely not en route to a seaside resort (5, 4) and e) A tale of two cities. (6, 3, 5)

363. What was George Orwell's actual name? (4, 5)

364. In the spy/political thriller *The Ipcress File*: a) What actor played Harry Palmer? (7, 5) b) What character was the main "bad guy"? (5)

365. In *Where Eagles Dare*, who played the main character, Major Smith? (7, 6)

366. Which two Irish barristers should Donald Trump have sent for to defend him in the impeachment trial in the US Senate? (4, 6) and (7, 8)

367. John A. Costello and James Dillon, on their way to hand in their seals of office, declared how much they disliked public houses. a) Who, in the car, then said, "F***, I now know why we are going in this direction today and why we are out of touch with the people." (7, 7); b) In what year did this conversation take place? (4)

368. Name four politicians (no duplication), whose surnames begin with the letter V: a) Ministers: 21st century. (8 and10)   b) Prime Ministers: one in the 20th century and one in the 21st century. (8 and 8)"

369. In the 2020 Irish general election, which two constituencies did not return any FF or FG deputies? (9-6) and (6, 5-7)

370. In 2020, in which constituency was no deputy elected, apart from FF and FG? (4, 5-4)

371. Like for MM in Ireland, match the following Prime Ministers with the correct EU country (Feb. 2021): KK _____ (7) MM _____ (6) JJ _____ . (8)

372. Presidents: One past, one present, beginning with the letter Z. (4, 8)

373. Election-winning party in 2021: TEDVSNOVEEJE (12); In what country? _____ (6)

374. Lindsay Graham is the senior senator for South Carolina. a) name a famous fictional senator for South Carolina; (4 or 9, 6)   b) In what book and film? (6, 3 ,7) c) The author? (5, 5)

375. Not Armani, but 'gave it a lash' in Germany in 2021. (5, 7)

376. Arguably, he saved the Euro, but will he manage Italy? (5, 6)

377. Presidents, Premiers or First Ministers: get a Chancellor that mattered in his time: (6) _____ Sturgeon; (6) _____ Bhutto; (7) Mary _____ ; (8) Margaret _____ ; (8) _____ Merkel; (6) _____ Rousseff. (5)

378. High English legal officer also a master baker? (6, 2, 3, 5)

379. The White House in Africa! (10)

380. The development of the atomic bomb: a) name of project? (9)   b) director of project? (11) c) location of project, either specific or US State name? (3, 6)

381. You might not have to read Michael _____ to feel or experience meritocratic hubris. (6)

382. Five US Presidents: Get a US State: (5) _____ Trump, _____ Jackson, Barack _____ , _____ Eisenhower, _____ Truman.

64

383. Elected past and present: New York, Kerry South, Cork North West; all the same? (8)

384. Across the water, they don't race inside it, but keep an eye on you, all the same.
(1, 1, 1, 1, 10)

385. One could be struck down with a bug from this place in England. (6, 4)

386. Sounded like he cleaned up in America in days past. (1, 5, 6)

387. This peer of the realm was not camera shy (4, 7)

388. Formerly Formosa. (6)

389. Predecessor of Suharto. (7)

390. Daughter of Ali Bhutto (Muslim forename only). (7)

391. "In the state of nature, the life of man is solitary, poor, nasty, brutish and short." The answer is a social contract for an absolute sovereign. Name the political philosopher. (6, 6)

392. Last President of Ceylon. (12)

393. "European presidents, premiers or equivalent: Costa, Bettel, Mattarella, Marin, Jansa, Frederikson:

get a) the country with the largest economy (5) and b) the most northerly country. (7)

394. Irish referenda: matters in issue? a) Narrowest majority in percentage terms 1995? (7)   b) Largest majority in percentage terms 1979? (8)

395. In Ireland, there have been nine referenda on EU-related issues. How many were passed at the first referendum on the issue presented? (4)

396. Who wrote biographies of: a) both Sean Lemass and Noel Browne; (4, 6) b) both John A. Costello and Eamon de Valera? (5, 9) c) of Patrick Hillery? (4, 5) d) of Peter Sutherland? (4, 5)

397. Military hero: "I shall return". (7, 9)

398. He used to rampage through foreign fields in his pomp. (4, 6)

399. Unlike Joshua, he did not blow the walls, but they came tumbling down anyway. (5, 8)

400. Between the wars, this gave Poland access to the Baltic. (3, 6, 8)

401-500

401. Was this Fianna Fáil TD (retired for some years), a member of the Church of Scotland? (6, 4)

402. Did he have a spring in his step? (9, 6)

403. This Western European country made Christmas Day an official holiday, as late as 1958. (8)

404. Which side of the "Borders" is Berwick? (choose between England and Scotland)

405. Not exactly Oxbridge, but west of the Bann, nonetheless. (5)

406. Not a Belfast-located academy, rather this academic location, east of the Bann, for what might have been euphemistically called political reasons. (9)

407. Did this Protestant roll out the barrel for the SDLP? (4, 6)

408. Like Selma to Montgomery, was this a bridge too far for "civil rights" up North? (10)

409. He had a dramatic escape from captivity, but was "hunted down" at Westminster. (5, 5)

410. He was an iconic 'loyalist' figure, who stood firm in a gale. (5, 6)

411. Now Russian, Kaliningrad was a German city of what name? (10)

412. What was capital of the "Federal Republic of West Germany"? (4)

413. Did this Italian-sounding work from 1957 make French cows more productive? (3, 6, 2, 4)

414. In 1967, Glasgow Celtic were certainly not of a mind for what would be named there some forty years later! (3, 6, 6)

415. If the Tory party is the Church of England at prayer, or indeed the reverse, what is, or at least was until recently, the Republican/GOP equivalent? (12)

416. Usually, but certainly not always, not a good London address for spendthrifts to reside in. (2, 7, 6)

417. State Department "royalty" for U.S. in lead up to the Vietnam war? (5, 5, 5)

418. Did some people think some decades ago that this prominent Irish politician had taken out North Vietnamese citizenship? (6, 5)

419. Men wear veils and women do not among what African people, also known as "Blue Arabs"? (7 or 6) both are correct.

420. He and AK would have different priorities each dawn. (5)

421. A "tricky" and "wet" entrance some decades ago. (9)

422. Will the Healy-Raes note this Kerry on climate change? (4)

423. Havel and Klaus, more in common than a country or a Presidency. (6)

424. Who said in January 2021 "and the key thing is we've got our fish back. They're now British fish and they're better and happier fish for it." (5, 4-4)

425. Fianna Fáil got 77 seats in 1933, 1938, 1989, and in _____ . (4)

426. Fine Gael got 31 seats in 1948 and in _____ .(4)

427. When the Gardaí came to arrest Charles Haughey in 1970, what prominent public figure, it was said, was visiting his house? (5, 5)

428. Robert Abela came after Joseph _____ in Malta, (6) but will Bobi _____ come after Yoweri Museveni in Uganda? (4)

429. Recently published about his life in "loyalism", and written with a co-author. (5, 10)

430. A _____ in Kildare South, and _____ in Cork South-West. (5, 5)

431. A Cumann na nGaedheal Minister, a modern minister for Public Expenditure and Reform, and a current Independent TD, forenames only. (3), (7), (6)

432. Re-took office in 2018 aged over 90:   a) Who? (8, 7) b) In what country? (8)

433. Failed assassinations: Get a long standing EU policy: (3)   Pope_____VI; (4)
_____ Navalny; (6) _____ De Gaulle. (7)

434. Congresswoman Marjorie Taylor _____ would not be a normal _____ , would she?
(6 and 5)

435. Currently (forenames only), a TD south of the Shannon (2); two Senators (4), (4) and one from Dublin in a Parliament somewhere else. (5)

436. Sinn Féin got 37 seats in 2020, and Labour got 37 seats in _____ . (4)

437. Egyptian leaders, get the power in a neighbouring area: (5) _____ Fattah al-Sisi; Anwar _____; Gamal _____ Nasser; _____ Mubarak; Mohamed _____ .

438. A rose in Mayo, but in Cavan-Monaghan it is _____ . (7)

439. *The Decline of the West* author. (6, 8)

440. This country was not ruled by a blacksmith. (8, 8)

441. He got his Irish sounding 'nickname' from his mother's side. After his death, this name gained worldwide iconic status. (3)

442. Did she have an Oscar in the 19th century? Known in literary circles as _____ . (8)

443. William and Michael _____ : an Upper House family. (5)

444. Nearly three centuries ago, he made "a modest proposal." (8, 5)

445. This Scots/Canadian economist was no "big deal" in "affluent" America, and yet _____ . (4, 7, 9)

446. A schism dating from A.D. 632. (5, 4)

447. The body of a former Italian Prime Minister was found in the boot of a car. (4, 4)

448. This former Italian Prime Minister was noted for having a high degree of "plasticity". (6, 10)

449. Southern Italy is commonly known as _____ . (11)

450. Was he a "Kapital" influence on Marx? (6)

451. Was it intent on their part to lie down? (3,7)

452. A saline solution to urban development in the USA? (4, 4, 4)

453. A good while ago now, from the Midlands, he could sound as if he was awfully holy. (6, 1, 8)

454. Not the boys of Kilmichael, but from not too far away. (3, 5, 4)

455. Up North, he had a tough hill to climb, almost every day. (6, 6)

456. Some 50 years ago, she made a spectacle of him:
a) Who was the subject? (10, 6) b) Who was the
object? (8, 8)

457. Alberto (later jailed) had been President of this
South American country. Daughter Keiko failed
to be elected in 2021. a) surname (8), (b) country.
(4)

458. Was this lad the son of Stevie the Sassenach? (6, 11)

459. He brooked no interference from the natives. (13)

460. This man, reared in Galway, became infamous in
his day; not really a bag of laughs. (7, 5)

461. Usually about 11.00 am on weekday mornings, he
did not talk "pie in the sky". (4, 7)

462. This English journalist sounds like a peaceful
man. (6, 6)

463. Did this former Prime Minister, once the leader
of IRGUN, get a good start? (8, 5)

464. He sounds like a relation of John Hume, but far
from it. (4, 7-4)

465. Was this "Boer warrior" and "philosopher about
Hungary" listed in the "ourselves alone" almanac?
(6, 8)

466. The Boris _____ (4) is child's play compared with Charlie at _____ . (9)

467. Is this knight of the realm averse to using cheques or credit cards? (3, 7, 4)

468. Annalena _____ , used to trampolines, would be well able to ride "bareback." (8)

469. His (British) broadcasting gravitas held the kingdom in thrall on great occasions of church and state. (7, 8)

470. These two sons of the above (forenames only), were, at the least, "chips off the old block". (5, 8)

471. These sons of Irish fathers were also chips off the old block: a) Academic politics (5, 7) b) Newspaper ownership; (6, 2, 6) c) Sports broadcasting. (4, 1'5)

472. Once upon a time, Boris Johnson was thinking 'straight', but would these current politicians think 'straight' on the product? (6):
Andy _____ (7), _____ Blinken (6), _____ Rabbitte (4), _____ Laschet (5), Hildegarde _____ (8), Malcolm _____ . (6)

473. Who once said: "The seventies will be socialist"? (7, 6)

474. Would you play bridge with _____ ? (5)

475. Who promoted politically the "white heat of technology"? (6, 6)

476. Would you, in his time, have played "snap" with _____ . (2, 6)

477. Decided to step down during Ramadan 2021? Reflect on first letters of Lent, Easter, Ramadan, Eid, Advent, Nollag. (6)

478. Would you play *pétanque* or *boules*, tête à tête with _____ ? (2, 3)

479. Across the pond, while centuries old, these states are also "new": (4), (6), (9), (6)

480. Martin _____ failed in 2017, but Olaf _____ came first in 2021. (6 and 6)

481. Answer more literary than political (3, initials only): _____ Wallace; (3) Wallis _____ ; (7) _____ Wallace. (6)

482. Not Laurence in Dublin long ago and did not win in Canada in 2021. (4)

483. Widely acclaimed as one of the great editors of his era, before a Mr Murdoch came to town. (6, 5)

484. Former Irish Times columnist more contrarian than Eamonn Dunphy!! (4, 6)

485. James Plunkett showed the Dublin of Larkin and Murphy in a very poor light. (8, 4)

486. Herbert Morrison's grandson. (5, 9)

487. Is this chap half mad? (6)

488. Malcolm McArthur had a "pilot's view" from this chap's residence. (7, 8)

489. She sounds like she was like a city chief, but was in fact a head of government. (5, 4)

490. If the French gave us the *chaise longue*, the Turks gave us this _____ ? (3, 7)

491. *Darkness Before Noon* author. (6, 8)

492. The two African colonies of Portugal. (6, 10)

493. A long-time leading politician (CSU) in Bavaria from the 1950's to the 1980's. (5, 5, 7)

494. In all fairness – according to this literary masterpiece – one often, but not always, follows

the other: a) the book (5, 3, 10) b) the author. (6, 10)

495.   Name four Irish Presidents who served two full terms. (1'5), (2, 6), (7), (8)

496.   In the 1980s, was this Secretary of State contrary to expectations? (9, 4)

497.   The two African tribes that were victims of German genocide in the early 20th century? (6, 4)

498.   Not the Irish IDA, but the prominent president of the Madrid region? (6, 4, 5)

499.   Name a member of the Biden-appointed cabinet that begins with the letter Y; (6) with B; (7) with A; (6) and with W. (5)

500.   Name six Taoisigh that did not represent Dublin constituencies. (6) (5) (5) (6) (8) (5)

SECTION TWO: SOLUTIONS!

SOLUTIONS
001-100

Solutions: 01-100

1. 'Crown'

2. Rabbitte

3. a) Conor Cruise O'Brien; b) Kwame Nkrumah; c) Accra

4. Lagarde

5. The White House

6. Bernard

7. Julian

8. George Blake

9. Ross

10. Lam

11. Umunna

12. Labour (O'Toole, Brenda, Una, Áine, Lara, Robert)

13. Margaret Thatcher

14. Joan of Arc

15. Lisa Chambers

16. David Norris

17. Michael Foot

18. Neil Kinnock

19. Modi

20. John Maynard Keynes

21. Maréchal

22. WHO (Oliver, Hanna, Wera)

23. Anne Boleyn

24. Jody (print journalist); Adam, Wolf; Marr (TV)

25. Anneliese

26. Harold Wilson

27. Coughlan, Desmond, O'Leary

28. Crossman, Crosland

29. Abiy Ahmed

30. "Seville"

31. John Profumo

32. Louis Mountbatten

33. Nevada

34. Bacik

35. The Kray twins

36. Fine Gael (Emily, Newton, Isabel, Finlay, Eoghan, Gene, Andrew, Laura)

37. Anthony Blunt

38. Regina

39. Fergus Finlay

40. 'Boxer'

41. The Kennedys

42. Leo Tolstoy

43. Fillon

44. Schmidt, Kohl

45. William Rowan Hamilton

46. Pence

47. William Butler Yeats

48. Carey, Kennedy, O'Neill, Moynihan

49. George Bermingham

50. "To be or not to be"

51. Cowen

52. Ben Dunne

53. Andropov-Chernenko

54. Brooke

55. Moon

56. West Belfast

57. Goldwater

58. Rudd

59. Robinson

60. Troy

61. Reagan Democrats

62. Ladybird Johnson

63. Gordon Brown

64. Eisenhower

65. Leopold Bloom

66. Hermann Goering or Hermann Göring

67. Emmanuel Macron

68. IPA: (Ian, Peter, Arlene)

69. Dillon

70. Nicola Sturgeon

71. Herbert Hoover

72. Keir Hardie

73. Alan, Tom.

74. Evita

75. Leinster House

76. Garibaldi

77. Pope

78. Martin: (either forename or surname of all nine politicians)

79. Gerald Ford

80. Prince Charles

81. John F. Kennedy

82. Basil Chubb

83. Caravaggio

84. Forza Italia

85. Cousins

86. John Rawls

87. "The absence of co-operation".

88. John Bruton

89. Enoch Powell

90. Gallagher

91. Joe

92. Tbilisi

93. Munster

94. The Pentagon

95. My Lai

96. The domino effect

97. Henry Kissinger

98. The Tallaght Strategy

99. a) Internal, b) North-South, c) East-West

100. Ernest Blythe

SOLUTIONS
101-200

! Solutions: 101-200

101. Putin

102. *Towards a Just Society*

103. Chu (Ursula, Coveney, Harris)

104. John Kelly

105. Susan Denham

106. "communist"

107. Heffo's army

108. Rugby

109. "The Long Fellow"

110. McGillicuddy

111. "The Big Fellow"

112. Paine: (A, Patrick, Extinction, Irish, National)

113. Reynolds, O'Malley.

114. Duda

115. The Sioux

116. The Bay of Pigs

117. Picard: (David, Peston, Ryan, Amanpour, Iain, Claire)

118. Douglas Gageby

119. *Chicago Daily Tribune*

120. Alfie Byrne

121. Castlebar

122. Denning

123. Michael, Leo, Eamon

124. John Law

125. Grattan's Parliament

126. Friedrich von Hayek

127. Thekla Beere

128. David Ben Gurion

129. Chaim Herzog

130. Moshe Dayan

131. The Sallins Train Robbery

132. Skinner

133. Edward Heath

134. a) Raisa Gorbachev; b) Reykjavik

135. Woodward and Bernstein

136. Ben Bradlee

137. Detta O Cathain

138. DB (David Byrne)

139. Denis Healey: Geoffrey Howe

140. Preston

141. Hales: (Lukashenko, Eamon, Hogan, Sunak, Abe 1)

142. a) 1973, b) 2020 c) 2002 d)1965

143. Shinwell

144. Orban

145. Macau: FAO, NATO, UNICEF, IMF, OECD

146. a) Donald J. Trump, b) Charles J. Haughey

147. Jacques Delors

148. Denmark

149. Gooks

150. The Hanoi Hilton

151. Robert McNamara

152. Mary Lou

153. Glasnost

154. John Mackintosh

155. a.) The Gutenberg Printing Press, b) Gestetner

156. Rerum Novarum

157. Seville

158. Thomas Mann

159. James Carville

160. Shah of Iran

161. Bashir al Assad

162. Suez canal

163. Quebec

164. Pandit Nehru

165. Rudyard Kipling

166. Tartus

167. Latakia

168. Alamite

169. Sciences Po

170. Ecole Nationale d'Administration

171. Trinity College, Dublin

172. The Doctrine of Precedence

173. Finisterre

174. Bob Hawke

175. Fordism

176. Nasser

177. Golan

178. Tripoli

179. F.W. de Klerk

180. Harvard

181. Mexico

182. Finian

183. Tipperary

184. Jim Crow

185. Neil Blaney

186. Peter Barry

187. Peter Brooke

188. Baton Rouge

189. Mitt Romney

190. CIA

191. Edmund Burke

192. Juncker

193. Cosgrave

194. Hillery

195. Robin, Eagle

196. The State Department

197. Dukes, Cox

198. *Frankfurter Allgemeine Zeitung*

199. Gerhard Schröder or Gerhard Schroeder

200. Alan Rushbridger

SOLUTIONS
201-300

Solutions: 201-300

201. *Belfast News Letter*

202. *The Belfast Telegraph*

203. *The Irish News*

204. St Augustine

205. St Thomas Aquinas

206. Constantine

207. Ludwig Erhard

208. Georges Pompidou

209. King Juan Carlos

210. Paschal Donohoe

211. Jeremy Bentham (or Thomas Malthus)

212. a) *The Wealth of Nations*, b) Adam Smith

213. Vincent Browne

214. *Hot Press*

215. *Private Eye*; "Dear Bill"

216. Michael O'Hehir

217. John Bowman

218. Peter Snow

219. Lester Pearson

220. Adolf Eichmann

221. Simon Wiesenthal

222. Reinhard Heydrich

223. Confucius

224. Han

225. *The Devlin Report*

226. Arthur Scargill

227. Cormac Breslin

228. Brexit

229. Christy Ring

230. 'Paddy the Plasterer'

231. Plato: (Patrice, Olaf, Trotsky, Archduke, Lincoln)

232. Delaware

233. Sean Loftus

234. John Nott (or Noel Dorr)

235. Walter Cronkite

236. Alistair Cooke

237. The Hurlers on the ditch

238. Rory O'Hanlon

239. Willie Whitelaw

240. Norman Tebbit

241. Frances Condell

242. McGee

243. James Connolly

244. Roger Casement

245. Lloyd George

246. Karachi

247. Islamabad

248. East Pakistan

249. a) *The Making of the President*
    b)Theodore H White

250. Archbishop Mannix

251. Ned Kelly

252. Paul Keating

253. Berlin

254. Patrick Pearse

255. S (ie. John Smith) (i.e. Sequence is Starmer,
    Corbyn, Milliband, Brown, Blair, Smith)

256. Donald Dewar

257. Aneurin Bevan

258. Nelson McCausland

259. *Parnell and his Party*

260. Priti

261. Boss Croker

262. Al Smith

263. Butte

264. Jim Dooge

265. Sykes/Picot

266. Mossadegh

267. Shirley Temple Black

268. Rasputin

269. John Wilkes Booth

270. Thomas a' Becket

271. The Jackal

272. Graham Greene

273. Mark Rutte

274. Sovereign Wealth Fund

275. Lenin

276. Schleswig Holstein

277. Chequers

278. The Cortes

279. The Elysée Palace

280. Papa Doc Duvalier

281. Rafael Trujillo

282. Jacinda Ardern

283. Scott

284. John

285. a) Sutherland, b) Okonjo-Iweala

286. Rand Paul
     (Ree, Allen, Neagh, Derg)

287. Colum Eastwood

288. a) Frost, b) Jingping

289. Sturgeon and Salmond

290. The Fabian Society

291. Bismarck

292. Richard Titmuss

293. Doug Beattie

294. Mise Éire

295. Cornelius Ryan

296. Boyne: Byrne; Corrib: Connolly; Liffey outside
     Dublin; Lawless; Dargle: Donnelly

297. Réunion

298. Sean Flanagan

299. 'The Cope'

300. Avril Doyle

SOLUTIONS
301-400

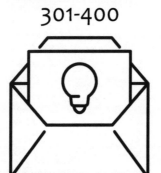

Solutions: 301-400

301. Des Foley

302. a) Belgium, b) Waterloo

303. Hackett

304. Walter Ulbricht

305. Christopher Ewart-Biggs

306. The Europa

307. Jeffrey Donaldson

308. Eddie McAteer

309. Gerry Fitt

310. Garvaghy

311. Tiede Herrema

312. 'Cash for ash'

313. Blair, Major

314. a) Chanakya b) *Arthashastra*

315. Portugal

316. Lemass

317. a) Erna Solberg, b) Sanna Marin

318. Monarchy, Belgium

319. Reg Empey

320. 2nd

321. a)Western Sahara, b) Sahrawi

322. ECJ
(Lemass, FitzGerald, Murphy ie. CHARLES Haughey, EITHNE FitzGerald, JOHN O 'Donoghue)

323. Kenny and Spring

324. Andrews

325. 1968

326. a) Svetlana, b) Zhukov, c) Georgy Malenkov

327. a) Randolph, b) Clementine, c) Blenheim Palace, d) Chartwell

328. Socrates

329. Karl Popper

330. Hess, Speer

331. Franco

332. Hassan

333. Prince Charles

334. a) Tet, b) Giap

335. Dien Bien Phu

336. Westmoreland

337. The Berrigans

338. Madame Nhu

339. Il Duce

340. Capitals

341. Nero

342. Archangel Gabriel

343. Pol Pot

344. The Spanish Inquisition

345. Albright

346. Fox

347. Khmer Rouge

348. Ernest Bevin

349. John le Carré

350. The Cheka

351. Anwar Sadat

352. Molotov

353. The Kenny Report

354. Denis Healey

355. a) Nagorno-Karabakh, b) Azerbaijan

356. Wahhabism

357. Aramco

358. MBS

359. The Religious Police

360. a) Cecil Woodham-Smith, b) F.S.L. Lyons

361. *The Big Wind*

362. a) Catalonia, b) Animal Farm, c) Nineteen Eighty-Four d) Wigan Pier, e) London, Paris.

363. Eric Blair

364. a) Michael Caine, b) Dalby

365. Richard Burton

366. John Rogers and Michael McDowell

367. a) Patrick Lindsay, b)1957

368. a) Villiers and Varoufakis, b) Verwoerd and Varadkar

369. Roscommon-Galway, Dublin South -Central

370. Cork North-West

371. Estonia, Poland, Slovenia

372. Zuma, Zelensky

373. Vetevendosje, Kosovo

374. a) 'Seab' or Seabright Cooley
b) *Advise and Consent* c) Allen Drury

375. Armin Laschet

376. Mario Draghi

377. Brandt : (Nicola, Benazir, Robinson, Thatcher, Angela, Dilma)

378. Master of the Rolls

379. Casablanca

380. a) Manhattan, b), Oppenheimer, c) Los Alamos or New Mexico

381. Sandel

382. Idaho – (Donald, Andrew, Obama, 'Ike', Harry)

383. Moynihan

384. G.C.H.Q. Cheltenham

385. Porton Down

386. J. Edgar Hoover

387. Lord Snowdon

388. Taiwan

389. Sukarno

390. Benazir

391. Thomas Hobbes

392. Banderanaike

393. Italy and Finland

394. Divorce, Adoption

395. Five

396. a) John Horgan, b) David McCullagh, c) John Walsh (same name, different authors)

397. General (or Douglas) MacArthur

398. Mike Pompeo

399. Ernst Honecker

400. The Danzig Corridor

SOLUTIONS

401-500

Solutions: 401-500

401. Seamus Kirk

402. Alexander Dubcek

403. Scotland

404. England

405. Magee

406. Coleraine

407. Ivan Cooper

408. Burntollet

409. Airey Neave

410. Gusty Spence

411. Konigsberg

412. Bonn

413. *The Treaty of Rome*

414. *The Lisbon Treaty*

415. Evangelicals

416. 11 Downing Street

417. Henry Cabot Lodge

418. Ruairi Quinn

419. Touareg or Tuareg

420. Sunak

421. Watergate

422. John

423. Vaclav

424. Jacob Rees-Mogg

425. 1997

426. 2002

427. Brian Walsh

428. Muscat, Wine

429. Billy Hutchinson

430. Berry, Holly

431. Joe, Michael, Mattie

432. (a) Mahathir Mohamad; (b) Malaysia

433. CAP (Paul, Alexei, Charles)

434. Greene and Green

435. Pa, Mark, Paul, Clare (that is, Daly)

436. 2011

437. Hamas (Abdel, Sadat, Abdel, Hosni, Morsi)

438. Heather

439. Oswald Spengler

440. Southern Rhodesia

441. Che

442. Speranza

443. Yeats

444. Jonathan Swift

445. John Kenneth Galbraith

446. Sunni: Shia

447. Aldo Moro

448. Silvio Berlusconi

449. Mezzogiorno

450. Engels

451. The Bedouin

452. Salt Lake City

453. Oliver J. Flanagan

454. The Healy Raes

455. Seamus Mallon

456. a) Bernadette Devlin, b) Reginald Maudling

457. a) Fujimori, b) Peru

458. Sean MacStiofain

459. Brookeborough

460. William Joyce

461. Adam Boulton

462. Jeremy Paxman

463. Menachem Begin

464. Alec Douglas-Hume

465. Arthur Griffith

466. Flat, Abbeville

467. Sir William Cash

468. Baerbock

469. Richard Dimbleby

470. David and Jonathan

471. a) David Farrell, b) Vivion de Valera, c) Tony O'Hehir

472. Banana: (Burnham, Antony, Anne, Armin, Naughton, Noonan)

473. Brendan Corish

474. Trump

475. Harold Wilson

476. De Valera

477. Arlene

478. Le Pen

479. York, Jersey, Hampshire, Mexico

480. Schulz, Scholz

481. GBS (Ben, Simpson, George)

482. Erin

483. Harold Evans

484. John Waters

485. *Strumpet City*

486. Peter Mandelson

487. Maduro

488. Patrick Connolly

489. Golda Meir

490. The ottoman

491. Arthur Koestler

492. Angola and Mozambique

493. Franz Josef Strauss

494. *Crime and Punishment*, Fyodor Dostoevsky

495. O'Kelly, De Valera, Hillery, McAleese

496. Alexander Haig

497. Herero and Nama

498. Isabel Diaz Ayuso

499. Yellen, Blinken, Austen, Walsh

500. Martin, Kenny, Cowen, Bruton, Reynolds, Lynch

Acknowledgments

This book of quizzes, which originated in the friendly fire exchanged between two friends over an eighteen month period, would never have seen the light of day without the help and encouragement of a number of people. We would like to thank them all.

From the beginning, Tony Brown grappled with many of the proposed questions, offering valued opinion on the difficulties or otherwise of the quiz.

Liam Murphy generously examined, in detail, much of the material and offered important critical evaluation.

Stephen Collins's wisdom, encouragement and sound advice helped in defining the boundaries.

Clare Tuohy, while venturing the opinion that the quiz was "a mind game between Bourke and Scally", was supportive from start to finish.

A number of friends, at different turning points, provided just the right company to keep us to the task. Perhaps, unwisely, we did not always accept recommendations or advice, but very much valued their interest and support. Muiris FitzGerald went so far as to contribute a question. Responsibility for the final version of questions and solutions are ours alone.

The project would not have been completed without the editing flair and publishing expertise of Helena Mulkerns.

We are particularly appreciative of the contributions of Deirdre O'Hanlon and Dorothy Scally who put in the hard yards, with remarkable fortitude, of typing the manuscript, proofing, and correcting the errors.

Tim Bourke
William Scally

About the Authors

Tim Bourke worked as a senior executive in the agri-food sector and as a consultant in various areas of industry, together with educational and social research projects. He has also had a long term involvement in politics at academic, policy and grass roots level. An elite thinker, he passes much time observing and commenting on the machinations of humanity down the ages and across the continents. He enjoys nothing more than engaging with the great unknowns of the day. He delights in posing the abstruse question that requires an acrobatic mental agility to lead to the solution.

William Scally's working career spanned the semi-state corporate spectrum, the political arena, and working as policy adviser to various governments. He also worked as a public policy consultant and lecturer in adult education. A quintessential analyst and formidable interlocutor, he takes considerable pleasure in putting the knowledge quotient of family and friends on trial. That he has access to the solutions increases his enjoyment tenfold, as the quizzed strain their brains not alone to arrive at the answer but, frequently, to arrive at the very question.

LITTLEMORE PRESS, DUBLIN